AUCTION

PITT POETRY SERIES

TERRANCE HAYES
NANCY KRYGOWSKI
JEFFREY MCDANIEL
EDITORS

AUCTION

QUAN BARRY

UNIVERSITY OF PITTSBURGH PRESS

Published by the University of Pittsburgh Press, Pittsburgh, Pa., 15260
Copyright © 2023, Quan Barry
Manufactured in the United States of America
Printed on acid-free paper
10 9 8 7 6 5 4 3 2 1

ISBN 13: 978-0-8229-6717-0
ISBN 10: 0-8229-6717-0

Cover art: Do Ho Suh, *Specimen Series: 348 West 22nd Street, APT. New York, NY 10011, USA – Toilet, 2013.* Courtesy of the artist and Lehmann Maupin.
Cover design: Melissa Dias-Mandoly

For Wallace, who is everybody's friend—
with gratitude and admiration

Si je vaux quelque chose plus tard, je le vaux aussi maintenant! car le blé est le blé, même si les citadins le prennent, au début, pour de l'herbe.

If I am worth anything later, I am worth something now. For wheat is wheat, even if people think it is grass in the beginning.

—VINCENT VAN GOGH

CONTENTS

X

AUCTION

AUCTION

What was I wearing?

. . .

I don't recall.

. . .

I remember walking down a series of switchbacks
away from the Italianate mansion
where all of her children died.

. . .

Night was entering, inching over the world
horizontally from right to left, the moon's structured whiteness
an *objet d'art.*

. . .

Then we arrived at the beautiful space
filled with beautiful gold-flecked people.

. . .

Everywhere strings of light, illuminated filigree,
a world webbed with stars, the feeling of bodily effervescing.

. . .

No, I hadn't been to the track.

. . .

I'd heard that was where squalor lived,
a barely contained seediness that was allowed.

. . .

I am one who has been reared to prefer the cultivated,
even the men trailing with push brooms
in tuxedoes as they sweep up the bready droppings

that break apart so easily,
loosing their fragrance of grass and earth.

. . .

Why should this veneer fail me now?

. . .

Watching the crowd lean forward, smelling their hunger,
the sound of the gavel falling like a cudgel on a head,
and the good people rushing forward
to shake the hand of the victorious.

. . .

I saw our history in it,
roped right there in the ring.

. . .

The muscled beauty of excellence, the monocular acuity,
how the breadth of the eye
evolved for speed.

. . .

It stood on the dais as the groom lovingly turned
its best side to the light, its best side
being every side, coat gleaming like blackest water.

. . .

The whole room instantly aroused—
the men's pants tenting, the women with their sudden secretions
as happens when you are in the presence
of the holiest of forms.

. . .

It was looking at us with an awareness beyond time,
casting its fifty-foot parabolic gaze
broadly over the earth.

. . .

Admittedly, as my mind filled with images
of heated brands and whips, I thought of Christ last,
the petals of blood licking His face.

. . .

It was every being who has ever stood centerstage in chains—
all of us implicated simply by being there
regardless of sympathy or intent.

. . .

Ecce homo.

. . .

Then I heard a voice shout "2.2"
and another go higher.

. . .

The most pragmatic teaching Jesus ever gave:
render unto Caesar what is Caesar's,
render unto God what is God's.

. . .

The gavel finally falling on 2.8 million.

. . .

But what if we don't know the difference?

. . .

No, it wasn't just my presence
that made me a participant to spectacle, which explains
why I've carried this haunting ever since.

. . .

He said the poor will be with us always,
and I ran with it—I let it
let me off the hook.

. . .

Then the groom, tuxedo dark as ink,
himself descended from such brutality,
turned and led it out.

NEO-COLONIALISM

After she screamed, in an act of transference
the German took a folding chair into the ocean
and flicked it onto the beach. A small crowd formed.
Earlier I saw a man without any hands
carrying firewood down the strip, his arms
perfectly flat at the wrists as though the devices
had been knifed clean off. The plot
finally got to me and I went to interpolate,
join the crowd. It was a medusa, the iridescent lobe
of its genital-less body the size of a small dog—
it was at once translucent and opaque, metaphor
and thing-in-itself, its frayed tentacles
still stimulated, writhing, and we all stood there
watching its gelatinous throes, its thematic structure
water-dependent, dying, the thing a society, millions
of individuals forming an integrated self.
Local vendor #67 asked us why we landed it.
Previously that summer her hat blew off
but one of us heroically brought it back.

LIVING FOSSIL, LIVING GOD

Admittedly, there is something about its face,
the boxy pugilistic snout, the prehistoric eyes
that seem to stare down through

80 million years back to the very days of T-rex.
Though taxonomically the frilled shark is no snake
cutting through the lightless waters 5,000 feet down,

the creature looks to be the very essence
of the reptilian brain—cold-blooded, beyond
even the crocodile, that seemingly soul-less

armory of plates, a creature grounded wholly in the now
with no inner life beyond the moment. What would it be
to be this presence skirting through the dark

with its rows of teeth, a consciousness beyond mind
that watches what mind does, its sorrows,
a being that grows its young for three and a half years

in the dark night of its belly, the longest gestation
of any in the animal kingdom, and how it only comes to us
from time to time, pulled up in some fisherman's net

for all to behold the undying wonders of the sea?
To have lived on into the anthropocene,
this creature mostly blind, simply structured, unchanging,

feeding on small squids and fishes, others of its kind—
please don't misunderstand. I believe God does not exist
in time, but because we do, we cannot understand It.

But imagine eighty million years, passing second by second.
When I look at this silvery beast, I see God.

KEUR MOUSSA

All week with the Larium dreams—
dreamscape after dreamscape, each one
vivid as actual living.

. . .

Mornings I would wake
as though I'd never slept.
Each night lying down to a second life,
another world where decisions
had to be worked out, sorrows accepted.

. . .

Then it was Sunday.

. . .

In the Novotel, Masser seeing my tiredness,
my being tasked with two lives, asked
if I still wanted to go.

. . .

Wow, I said.

. . .

On the way out of the city
the talibés in their Western cast-offs
with their buckets in hand, some as young as four,
these littlest beings sent out into the streets
in the name of the Almighty.

. . .

When do we need to ask more
of tradition? How do I say no?
And is it that simple, or is there another side to this?

. . .

Like the child at the beach, not knowing what he wanted,
which was possibly just a friend
to guard his filthy clothes as he swam.

. . .

Then on into the countryside, everywhere the baobob
millennial, a feeling as if you should fall down
on your knees and press your face
into their roots.

. . .

Finally we pulled into the Abbey.

. . .

Instantly I was among the people
in their waxed fabrics, the women's headscarves
the jeweled colors of the most beautiful insects,
the iridescent kind that are every color in the sun.

. . .

There was a canopy, musicians, a dais.
I saw guitars, a drum set, amplifiers,
these children the beloved of Africa
sitting still in the July heat.

. . .

I turned to Masser.
This isn't what I'm looking for.
He nodded and disappeared.

. . .

Sundays Mimi and I would drive
the thirty minutes down from Death's Door
to St. Rosalia's, Star of the Sea.

. . .

Summers the parish swelling with summer people
so that the diocese would bring in extra priests
from the developing world.

. . .

Father Chester always promising
the mass is never ended. How he died alone
in a small room as orchestrated by his order.

. . .

Today is Easter Sunday. That's why I'm writing this.

. . .

Because I miss the brunches after mass
in that tiny blue house with the Bavarian trim
that my grandfather built on the lake.
From the second pew, gazing up at that figure
whose story I didn't believe in.

. . .

The water nymph Rusalka is wrong.
If He is dreaming of me, let Him never wake.

. . .

Finally Masser came back, nodded for me to follow.

. . .

I got up out of my plastic chair, the mass in full swing,
the music mixing in a sound board before pouring out
to the people swaying, arms alight.

. . .

We walked the grounds
down a path wide enough for cars
to the other side of the *terroir*
until we came to it.

. . .

The entire wall behind the altar adorned
with African figures and geometric designs,
the people painted like black lightning bolts,
their bodies slashes—

. . .

I am a movement and a stillness

. . .

—and the instrumentation,
the *kora* like a heavenly voice from the days of the prophets,
perhaps Michael himself alighting from the skies
with this three-foot long stringed calabash
to accompany what he had to relate.

. . .

From what I could tell the people crammed in that small clean space
were mostly tourists.

. . .

Like me, they didn't come here to see how the Senegalese
worshipped, that other space with the electric guitars
and the few hundred local people
rippling in the sun.

. . .

We came to hear the mass in Wolof, to hear the instruments
made of gourds and animal skins.

. . .

Why? What was so complicated about my life
I thought I could only find true fellowship here
and not across the meadow in the clearing?

. . .

Sometimes I still crave it.

. . .

Two days ago I pull up a Tenebrae
service on YouTube, listen to the white priests sing
they gave me vinegar to drink when I was thirsty.

. . .

What am I writing my way toward?
Release? Damnation? Or is damnation
a kind of release, the way you're left
no longer awaiting the worst?

. . .

Have you ever failed a child face-to-face
up-close and personal?

. . .

No one would ever accuse me of such a thing
because in this terrible world I did
what 98% of the population would have done—
I was drowning and I chose me.

. . .

Now at night I tape my lips shut.

. . .

Perhaps we are all just looking for the honey
the fathers bottle from the bees they keep.

. . .

In Greece, the wealthy dead were sent home from battle
embalmed in it.

. . .

Afterward I went looking for him. The small figure
peering over the fence, perhaps asking me to come and play.

. . .

Who are you, 2 persons in 100? The ones who hear a story on the radio
and pick up the phone, change a life? Who see it through
to the crushing end, the self on fire, the debrided skin
so tight you can't breathe?

. . .

And I found him. I was given a second chance.
Beside the Atlantic we played with the soccer ball
made of old clothes and duct tape.

. . .

I had just turned 44. In the gift shop I bought the honey,
a CD of the fathers and their instruments
from the days of Christ.

. . .

What I now believe. This world is an illusion,
just not the kind you think.

. . .

If he's dreaming of me, let him wake.
That's what Rusalka wrongly begs of the moon.

. . .

And if I woke up now? All this sorrow would disappear.
No need for all this seeking, these empty and utterly human attempts
to build a perfection among the detritus.

. . .

At the end of the Tenebrae service, there's a moment called *strepitus* (great
    noise),
each candle blown out, then the sounds of breakage. Floods.
Chaos in the dark. The moment the earth convulsed.

. . .

Some say it may have originated simply as a sign to depart.

APARTMENT A, UNIT 2

—after Do Ho Suh

That place on the bottom of any sandy lake
where sometimes I see it in the 30-odd seconds
I can go without breathing, there undulating
among the lake grass, this silent presence,
how this is just another way to think of it, this
the apartment's equivalent—what it looks like
when the refrigerator leaves its own body, the afterimage
as even an appliance is allowed to remember
that once it was infinite
and still is, home like a medusa, that ghostly lantern
pulsing in the dark, the things we see
in the first moments after we pull the cord
and throw the world into night: this house is souled,
this room is souled, this toilet souled, the stove
souled, beyond good and evil, beyond the body's
steel and glass, beyond even the metaphor of the soul
as a pillar of light, as a thing we can only intuit,
pray we have.

BY THE SHORE OF LAKE MONONA, THIS IS WHAT I HEARD

May all achieve equilibrium,
may all have access to the tools
to acquire equilibrium
like the story of his first day in town,
the young monk walking by an ATM
which emits a small sound as he passes,
the sound as if the machine
is greeting him, saying *welcome, stranger!*
the first in that foreign place to do so.
In turn the monk bows to the machine,
silently sending *mettā* its way,
loving kindness, that it may know peace
and be serene in the world.
And so it goes. Each time the monk passes
he wishes the small contraption ease,
then one day while making his rounds
he hears a beep, looks to see a bill
suddenly hanging from the machine's
steel lips. We must not lose sight
of the oneness in all things. Per-
severe. The monk bows deeply.

IN THE FAMILY

There was so much footage, too much or not enough depending
(technology!) and a difference of eleven hours, though in this way of
    being:
no now, no there, no here, no later

. . .

like the child who was strapped to the chair in the darkened room
for the first twelve years, how she never came to know
the concept of the interrogative, how pronouns work.

. . .

Compared to an adult, the brain of a three-year old
has twice the synaptic density. Over time,
the brain learning to prune itself, thin its connections
in a quest for efficiency.

. . .

The guru who is not a guru simply says we are like dogs
conditioned to bark. My words bring out the "X" in you,
your words bring out the "Y" in me.

. . .

Or imagine offering a newborn lamb to a predator who has not eaten
in many days. The conditions established for a mauling.
Blamelessness.

. . .

For example, is it snowing when you tell me I am not capable
of sustaining love, each flake papery
like a flower petal? Is it something about the grayness of winter?
Have we both had a good night's sleep?

. . .

What later became evident: by 5am Indochina time, the streets filled with
	saffron and plum,
whole oceans of color, each one signifying the specific tradition,
the subtle nuances in lineage.
	. . .

The first time I tuned in
I saw the formal invitation, his body asked
to come out into the light
and play.
	. . .

The regalia like a college graduation when the faculty processes into the arena
in their academic vestments, silly hats,
me always wondering
what university robes their graduates in salmon pink.
	. . .

Thankfully someone was whispering commentary, explaining
this is the Heart Sutra, the Heart Sutra the teaching that names the great
	nothing
at the heart of all things.
	. . .

Something about this rendition. It made me want to dance.
	. . .

I watched the journey across the grounds to the Full Moon Hall
of the one who was called Clear, Reflective Light; Meeting Spring; One
	Action;
of the Shakya clan in the family of the Buddha,
his body arranged on the litter and born aloft, treasured
in the place where he precipitated into form.
	. . .

Here the snow as petals from a begonia.
Something hand-made, artisanal, not capable
of permanence.
. . .

What I've seen of death: the way it can't help but happen to the face,
all tension gone, a collapsing around the mouth, a slackness.
No longer having to hold
oneself together.
. . .

Was that what the prisoner wanted? A return to infancy?
This man who killed his teenaged son
because the boy found the photos
of the man wearing diapers, engaging in one of the greatest of taboos.
. . .

The Greek for what the man was doing. Divorced of meaning,
to my ears the sound of the word as if describing
the state of being burnished, of bathing in first light.
. . .

When I looked it up, the image of a fly resting on a pile of dung.
In the animal kingdom, there are many
who draw sustenance this way.
. . .

Thay called it Interbeing, said death does not exist,
that we are merely points of light
along the spectrum.
. . .

In our family tree: animal ancestors, vegetable ancestors,
mineral ancestors.

. . .

Could this recognition be enough?

. . .

After the worst thing I have ever seen with my own eyes was seen
and I got off the phone with the police, Michael calling the FBI,
I didn't know what to do with it.

. . .

It was in those first days of the pandemic when we were all scrambling
for community, desperately turning to our screens
in lieu of home.

. . .

Through tears, I had to explain myself. There was an article in the *Times*,
I said.
I've never heard of zoom-bombing, the officer said.
He asked if I thought the worst thing I have ever seen with my own eyes
was happening in real-time.

. . .

Platelets. Needles. Columns. Rimes. When water droplets fall below
certain temperatures, ice
nucleates, snow falling like ripped paper, in turn, something precipitating
in us,
a recognition that our story of two people is no longer working.

. . .

I had never considered this. What would it mean to say
I was seeing the beginning, the first minutes
of a child's death?

. . .

Coprophagia. Two blue butterflies so beautiful their species is named
    for Adonis,
the insects photographed feeding on a lump of shit.

. . .

I have lived so long with these disparate stories raging inside my mind
that the world is at war again.

. . .

Or what the scene in *An Iliad* proves, the actor listing every conflict
since the time of the Akkadians,
a catalog of wars: we have never left it.

. . .

She was a toddler. No more than three. Her brain
presumably in the first stages of synaptic pruning,
this child I saw being savaged

. . .

and the conditioned were such
that there was nothing I could do.

. . .

From the proto-Germanic, Old Saxon, Old Norse, Swedish, Old
    Frisian, Dutch,
then perhaps the Old High German *skem*
which leads to *kem*, "to cover,"

. . .

how the word "shame"
precipitates down through the ages.

. . .

What I feel each time I open my eyes and see someone
in a state of suffering—the airport in Kabul, an infant handed over the wall,
the mother and children dead on the front page of the *Times*, killed
by Russian shrapnel, the pregnant women lifted
out of the rubble in Mariupol

. . .

and the feeling of shame at my helplessness, what the speaker said
at the march, that there would have been nothing we could do
had we been there in Minneapolis and watched the life
drain out of him in real-time

. . .

not like the child in therapy who after 9/11 draws a trampoline
in her picture of what she saw
so that those falling from the towers
might land safely ever after.

. . .

Friday one of the young activists says art is the space in which we imagine
what freedom might look like.

. . .

Imagination as agency.

. . .

Unfortunately for me, to be free means to be free of the one called
    Amy Quan.
It is not a particularly hopeful teaching,
but it is what this condition aspires to.
    . . .

Then conditions were such that I emailed Thay's poem to the list serve
as it was all said conditions could offer the group
in our collective pain.
    . . .

I am the twelve-year-old girl, refugee on a small boat,
    who throws herself into the ocean after being raped by a sea pirate,
    and I am the pirate, my heart not yet capable of seeing and loving.
    . . .

On the final day I watched as the casket was driven through the streets
    of Hue.
Thousands of people present at that early hour,
believers the world over, in Plum Village and beyond, prostrating
    themselves
at the passing of this incarnation of the embodiment of Love.
    . . .

What to wish for her, the girl child who was strapped to the chair
in the dark room for the first twelve years of her life?
    . . .

She's still alive
in a facility in California, having been failed
by all of us.
    . . .

Scientists believe the brain thins its connections in order to acquire
     language,
the ability to locate the self in the world.
. . .

Gone gone, all the way over, gone to the other shore.
. . .

What I wish for her sake: that in those first few years we are simply the
     Universe looking at itself
until someone rubs our cheek, kisses the top of our head
and points at the mirror, then something clicks
and we fall.

THE MAN ON THE TV IN THE BORDER TOWN SAYS HE FEELS NOTHING FOR THEM (PART 2)

When he said it, I actually gasped.
Like parts of a car, our bodies
were designed to be interchangeable.

In the event of the unfortunate, my eyes
could become his eyes, his heart
my heart, even this very minute

my blood could be coursing darkly
through his radial network of veins.
The Trappist monk who said

"If you believe in the incarnation of Christ,
then you must be willing to see His face
in anyone." I want to see His face, I need to see

His face in these days of closed fists
where the four chambers of the heart
clench the hours. What the darkness told me:

expand. Anger is the picking up
of a burning coal with the intent of hurling it
at the one you hate, said the Awakened One.

And so let me neither despise nor pity
you, man who professes to feel nothing
for the suffering of others.

Every afternoon there is a golden hour
as light angles itself perfectly through the atmosphere
burnishing the fields—

everything suddenly crowned
whether we like it or not.

POEM

Just two Saturdays ago I sat on Jan's living room floor
and demanded it, said I do not want
what the Buddha wanted for us, to live without suffering,
this edifying force as I believe the body needs to know
when it has been harmed, to know trauma

which if a color would be the same shade as blood pooled
under the eye, that I embrace pain because the universe is a wonder
and I will not deaden myself to anything, even the darkest dark,
which means even the photo of the young boy in the arms
of his smiling captors, how right there in the truck bed on a dusty road

in _____ one of them will take what the article describes as "a dull knife"
and like a violist sounding a long nocturnal note
saw the child's head off, knocking the air from my lungs
like the time I fell off a ladder, creating a vacuum at the center
of me as I had been doing with myself all summer,

me with the money and the time to learn to breathe
underwater, on my knees thirty feet deep in Mendota, my body
sheathed in two wetsuits, neoprene gloves and a hood,
twenty plus pounds cinched around my waist
to counter the buoyancy in an attempt to exhibit

competency at the basic skills such as taking my mask off
in 53° water with less than two-foot visibility,
the sudden cold like the back of a hand to the face,
causing the gasp reflex to kick in, the thrashing
like a beached fish as I breathe through both my regulator

and my nose, how I stay breathing like that, taking both air
and water into my lungs in equal measure only to learn
that Kim is right, that as long as I am also taking in air,
I can inhale water for a long time without dying,

I can live through this darkest dark, the two teenagers

in Janesville in full body armor with assault rifles
lurking at the edge of the protest and X saying
they put themself in between the crowd
and the teenagers and it was fine in the way things are fine
these days, in the way we all just keep going,

and so I remember that summer moment in the lake,
the way I kept going for one full minute, breathing in
these two contradictory elements, water and air, desperate
for the tiny piece of paper that would certify
I can do this, what we all do, day in, day out, living on

through the terrible wonder of what should be unlivable.

STILL, GIVE ME

all of it, even cruelty, the naked man
under the underpass on I-10 toward Houston,
his body twisted like an oak metastasizing
around a power line, and also the woman
panhandling by his side, the woman
working his deformity like an impresario
though sometimes we can only know
the surface and not the churning, the golden flecks
forming deep in the barrel, resulting in
my claiming both of them, yes, I pick
this man and this woman for my universe
not out of pity or *noblesse oblige*
but because they have *already* been chosen,
we are all the chosen, the universe looked deep
within its Unknowableness and we rose like cream
into being and then promptly forgot
what we are to each other: kin.
This is what it means to sin, to miss
the mark, to live as if we're not.

FOREWARD

Yesterday while skimming an article
on the 14 characteristics of such regimes,
I stumble on this description of fascism:

We no more saw it developing from day to day
than a farmer in his field sees the corn growing—
he simply wakes one morning to find it is over his head.

The way we allow things to take root,
each night silence sprouting in the earth
like the children's books I saw

in the *Heeresgeschichtliches*, Vienna's
military history museum, or the one in my dream,
on the cover a small flaxen-haired boy

somewhere in nature tending his geese
stands happily watching as the hooked-nose enemy
is marched out of town, the book titled:

"Das und Das Pocket Field Guide
to Occupied Lands" with an epigraph
from Dmitri Shostakovich:

there can be no music without ideology.
How the word "propaganda" comes from the world
of horticulture, to graft one plant onto another.

Dear reader: please forgive me
this tangent—the landscape of these alien fields
appeared so sweet, so contrary

to what I'd been told.

There can be no music without ideology.

–DMITRI SHOSTAKOVICH

THE LANDSCAPE OF THESE
ENEMY COMBATANTS

is the fastest way to recognize their incapacity for self-governance.
Too much green space, too many fountains, even the horse flies
allowed to drink from the well. And who knows what riches lie
untapped beneath their soil, in their cities whole districts
with their art deco façades still intact. Their agriculture unmodified,
their rivers undammed, it is a mystery they get anything done,
the top tax rate some astronomical percent even if the healthcare is free.

THE BIBLE OF THESE VULGARIANS

has only one tenet. For example, here is the parable of the failed suicide:
Someone wakes in the long night of the super moon, the black smoke
of fireworks shawling the sky. The pain so acute she feels it
in her hair, and so hand over hand she lets love's black rope
out from her heart and is healed. Everyone knows the true god comes with
    a sword
bulging in his mouth. Their god is the god of loose knots and weak beams.
Their god coos, "Good effort," and, "You'll get 'em next time, tiger!"

THE NATIONAL SPORT OF THESE DEGENERATES

involves water so that even newborn babies can participate.
There is no need to build stadiums or sign contracts, the rules always
in flux and nobody minds because in their tongue there are 29 words
for 'lovingly conducted sportsmanship.' When the national sport
is played at night, they find it even more beautiful, bodies remembering
how they came from the sea. Us, we never slept in the ocean. Our ocean
is for food and oil and refuse and conveyance, a vast nothingness to get
across.

THE SPACE PROGRAM OF THESE
REPROBATES

consists of Bertha, a single ship shaped like a giant egg
which their scientists annually encourage
local schoolchildren to decorate in pastels and stickers.
Nota bene: Bertha has never been anywhere.
Also, the bulk of their aeronautics program
focuses on mind training and breathing deep.
Learning to be happy with this world's endless frontiers.

THE LEGS OF THESE INFIDELS, OR, NOT TO PUT TOO CRUDE A POINT ON IT, THE ROSY FORK WHERE THEY MEET

as when a secondary queen goes out into the world
to make a new hive, how half the colony goes with her,
and in the interregnum, the bees temporarily massing
around their sovereign until the new palace is secreted.
Remember: the Greeks used honey to preserve their war dead
so that they could be sent home from battle daisy fresh.
It's the world's oldest cliché. Soldier, resist the sweetness.

THE EYES OF THESE CRAZED BELLIGERENTS

like mousetraps, like fishing nets, like one-way streets
backed up with traffic and no exit for miles. Don't be fooled.
Sometimes you can't see the thing until you're stuck ass-deep in it.
Remember the four cardinal points: from the north, chrysanthemums,
from the south, lilies, radiant orchids in the light of the east,
but in the western sun, every one a Venus fly trap, the red ovoid mouth
with its long sticky lashes set on kill.

THE SKIN OF THESE INCORRIGIBLES

will be the thing that makes you knock-kneed, this nation's pelts
that call to mind sugar still glittering in the cane. Know it is their weak spot,
the hours they spend oiling themselves until golden
as if preparing the body for the broasting pan, even the breasts
plump with fat, and the savor rising all the way to their godless heaven.
O sons of the motherland—one touch of their apple-tight skin
and instant blindness, webbed hands, hirsuteness, mongoloidism!

THE DREAMS OF THIS
BARBARIAN HORDE

are strangely dark given the race's other propensities.
Horse dreams, food dreams, dreams of the coming of weather.
Dream of the knife and dream of the rusty nail
and the dream of wielding them both against the neighbor.
Dream of the unending love. Dream of the one night stand.
Dream of the tongue on the mother's dirty nipple.
Dream of the hammer man coming to brick her in.

SURPRISINGLY, THE HEART OF
THIS BELLICOSE RACE

has a memory of crying one winter night, that it could be like this—
astral, two bodies communing in the non-physical realm. Lying on the red
    rug
for the first time in life she understands the limits of her nation's motto,
the law of the white dog in its cave of snow. Call it whatever you want,
this one-night insurrection, but be sure to advance with maximum heed
as the dog loves itself and will always survive. Remember, the master may
    be dead
but the mastered goes on with its icy fur frozen in a series of spikes.

SOLDIERS, DON'T FALL IN LOVE WITH THE PROFLIGATES OF THIS WORLD. CONSIDER

the children of such unions, their hearts misshapen, miscellaneously-lobed.
These women with their white sand ways, their breadfruit-aquamarine
   voices
that want to initiate you in their love sports. Instead, imagine a lemon
squeezed directly into your mouth, imagine sitting on a block of ice.
Even when she looks at you and you realize you could finally put down
the mantle you took up as a boy and be embraced for who you are—
in the name of God and country: loose not a single drop from your loins!

THE INSECURITIES OF THESE
BLOOD-THIRSTY SAVAGES

come from the usual place. "39 Ways to Make His Head Explode."
"Are Your Breasts Too Circular?" She knows she is a monster.
Hair everywhere and that dimple on her thigh so deep it tunnels
all the way to China. Not to mention the way she snorts in hot yoga,
giggling each time the yogi purrs, "Deepen your dog," or the way
she wants to name her only daughter 'Agony' just for the sound of it,
or the thing in the drawer of the nightstand that secretly keeps her sane.

THE METAPHORS OF THESE
STONE-AGE PRIMITIVES

are ship shape, moon tight, bottom fogged.
There is no metonymy as there are no substitutions
though a part for the whole is acceptable.
Pig-headed, bed of apples, ruined.
When she meets the enemy face to face,
she feels the trap door springing open to her heart.
Here, the cruelest month is loveless Friday.

THE BACKSEATS IN THE CARS
OF THESE TROGLODYTES

are covered in midnight-black naugahyde worn thin in spots.
You, as the sworn enemy of these people, should never feel
the upholstered seams imprinting on your naked buttocks,
but if you do, make your lovemaking a part of your warcraft.
Remember, only the females of mammals and nematodes, a phylum
of long cylindrical worms, have vulvas. Do whatever you have to do.
The most erogenous parts of the body are also the most vulnerable.

THE HANDS OF THESE BIG-
BOTTOMED IGNORAMUSES

are jumbo slabs of Sunday butter and your body the griddle.
Take but don't give. If the desire to reciprocate should arise, pick
the part of the body with the least nerve endings and lavish your
attention there. The teeth. The nail of the big toe. [Author's note: in the
Motherland, the woman receives pleasure just from fulfilling her
duty. In the shower I manipulate myself every third day. Whatever vigor
remains, I put to the war effort. I withdraw even in my mistress.]

46

THE BONES OF THESE
FUNDAMENTALIST D-BAGS

snap like chalk as you learn on the night you slam her against the wall
wanting to know who threw the grenade. Don't look at me. You're the one
whose schedule has become so predictable every kindergartener can set her
    watch
by your comings and goings. After it happens, set the bone yourself.
Use firewood if you have to. When you're done, hold her in your arms.
Feel her heart hammering as if a hummingbird were trapped in her ribs.
Whatever you do, don't tell her you're sorry. Don't feel sorry in the least.

THE TEARS OF THESE GLUTEN-
EATING PHILISTINES

disappear at first light. Each morning she gives you the widest smile,
still smiling even when you go away to "Bang-cock" on R&R.
Nothing sticks to them. Not like the time I was passed over
for commandant and I took out my weapon when I got home
and shot Mr. Kibb's, my kid's long-haired guinea pig, right through
    the eyes.
This time when we ghost there won't be folks holding onto helicopters.
This time we're not even taking the bomb-sniffing dogs with us.

THE MEDICINE OF THESE ARMPIT-STAINED BOTTOM FEEDERS

will, it's true, nurse you back to health after a friendly fire incident
in which you are left for dead, but soldier, always carry my words
in the pocket closest to your heart. When the war is over
will you be man enough to return here and claim your child,
the one with eyes like blackest almonds, who dreams nightly
of your return, on that day her mother with the shaved head
no longer a pariah among their people?

RESURRECTION THEORY

In the illuminated manuscript
several stained pages of naked women
lying on anvils—the metaphor
of the forge and the artisanal
as creation, always the smith
poised with his hammer and maul
over the reproductive organs,
the exempla of medieval fragments
& "the perils of Egypt"—the craftsman
who falls in love with his own skill,
consequently the prohibition
against the image because
to create is to become as god,
craft as divine erasure. The only poet
in the room, I sat and listened
and recognized. In Christology
the hypothesis that He was the son
of a smith and not a carpenter,
the generative symbolism of iron,
of smelting chaos into form.
We want to arise perfected from the grave.
I want this thing to go on after me.
Dead men throughe Hys myght
He raysed full sone agayne,
the alchemical tradition present
to some degree, the turning of detritus
into gold.

GOSHAWK

She said it was storming.
She had to move. After a decade
without doors, windows. Running out
into the white-capped world
toward the lashing
and then turning the corner.
The night the circus tent collapsed.
It was perched there on a rock,
glaring with its ripping feet.
Two animals recognizing each other as equals.
The nothing that is something
rose up in the air between them.
Most times transfiguration comes to us
well after the fact. Blood-heat. Lightning.
The canvas of the circus tent coming down
not like a parachute but a shroud.

UNREQUITED NOCTURNE

Heart first pricked by the foreignness
of your voice under the window
where I sleep by climbing
exactly two white stairs
up and up, a princess
without gradient or shadow.

. . .

Waves build on the ocean
in a way scientists don't understand,
the rogue wave compounding
out of nothing, seas flat as meadows.

. . .

It makes sense to me.
I forced myself to know you
and now I cannot not know—
a forty-foot wave hungering for something
to break on.

. . .

In the car on the way to the night lake
I tell the others. And so it originates.

. . .

Like sand in the oyster, laying down
the nightly bed of mother-of-pearl.
Heart all gunked up like a drain.

. . .

I could go on and on
about the fires and the golden apple
in all its litigious forbiddenness.

. . .

Why always gold?

. . .

But when I lengthened my head
to bite, what did you think I was doing?

. . .

On my way to you, it passed by on the left,
this luminous marauder I almost just hit with my windshield,
the owl sailing on the darkness
toward whatever, wings like sails in the doldrums.

. . .

Treed, I opened my eyes
and there you were, dawning.

. . .

O heart of glass
so the light prisms!
like Luciano & the morning star,
both Luciano & the morning star
bemoaning *if I can't, let nobody.*

. . .

Then everything becomes a game.
One hand held behind the back
while the other is effaced.

. . .

Or like the girl charging through the electric fence
to get to the one being gored,
beating the beast in the face with the pipe
like a prisoner quarrying stone.

. . .

Afterward I went and got the pillows
from your bed. Why not?
All the hair on the sill
documentation.

. . .

As if I were a bird or a thing
that nested. As if I had it to do all over again,
I would rebuild, help myself to whatever.

. . .

Now our wall has a door
that we meticulously do not open
as it's load-bearing—
without it, the world warps, a flat.

. . .

And so I go back
to a 24hr day, rolling in my own filth
like Thisbe with a sword through
the duodenum. Lion-judged.

. . .

Buddha says everything I am, beloved
& pleasing, will become otherwise, will become
separated from me. Does walking the roads below the goshawk,
imagining my shoulder ripped to the bone
count?

. . .

Saturday night in the field under the meteor shower,
I didn't answer when you asked.
The sky has been falling like this for millions of years.

. . .

You once said in music, rhyme is called melody.
Dissonance speaks for itself, the heart left
all thicket and gristle.

. . .

Exeunt.

. . .

Love like pulling the cord to a bare bulb.
I did this. I didn't do this. I did this. I didn't do this.

5 TIMES OUT OF 10, LOVE IS NOT ENOUGH

Yesterday gray skies, periodic rains
and now the earthworms are crisping
on the pavement, each one
no longer than a curl of macaroni,
the size an earthworm achieves
by April, not the fleshy ripeness
you see in August after a thunderstorm,
the nightcrawlers fat as human lips
wriggling on the concrete,
each long as my palm, long enough
that as a child I would sometimes
pick them up and ferry them
to the strip of grass between
the street and the sidewalk, a place
where they could sink back down
into the soggy dark, turning the earth
as they go, making it better,
and because empathy is not dead
though academics are starting to question it,
the way the catharsis empathy engenders
lets one off the hook—how easily we say
poor Trayvon, poor Tamir, poor Tyre, and leave it
at that, nothing changed, satisfied that we feel pain
at the reading of their names which proves
we are a loving person,
but I'm not ready to move on
from even these tiny beings littering the sidewalk,
each ring in their segmented bodies
with its own discrete heart.
I see them, imagine my own body desiccating
in the sun, my life-force drifting up
into the clouds where one day

it will come pouring back down
worthy to play its small part yet again
in this mess.

UNREQUITED NOCTURNE AS DREAM

Thirty years on and the shadow still in the garage,
still by the steps on the run that cut the yard on the diagonal.

. . .

I knew right then and there. You said this way was better.
Even the belief in nothing is a creed.
The desert opened its burnished gates, abiding.

. . .

Behind the woods of the religious school, the virgin
on the hill with her arms as if racked.

. . .

Someone was in the kitchen wasting water.
Someone wrapping potatoes in foil
and burying them in the flames. But the backdoor was open.
The black dog slipped out. The black dog
the first great love of my life.

. . .

Is this the dream of letting go?
Or just "I lose again."

. . .

How some of us practice on animals.

. . .

The poet-priest says it is right to love even when it is wrong.

. . .

Thrice-great Hermes watching from the lip of the bath.

. . .

I tell Mari the final question
I have dragged myself toward, the sound
of breath soughing. Everything ought to be
what it is, little intact heads, eyes agleam.

. . .

The way at this exact moment someone is sailing around the world
    solo.

. . .

Perhaps tellingly, the one thing in which I have achieved,
I discount.

. . .

Sometimes we say everything we need to say
without saying word one. Man puts his thoughts
in a jar and the jar in the ocean.

. . .

He did the best he could by me, offers the girl one table over
in the coffee shop, and so I come to my senses and erase the scene
with your drunken image, your bare feet cloven and furred.

. . .

You say I move as if there is some inaccessible room sealed off like a
    sepulcher
where the true treasure of the realm is kept shining in the dark.
There is no chamber of gold, I phonate, lying.

. . .

When I close my eyes,
a bottle bobs among the waves, a slip of paper furled in its belly,
the glass astonishingly green like the back of a housefly in sunlight.

. . .

Is it true? Cordage and groan, the uninterrupted wind
between continents. Does lasting satisfaction lie
in the climbing of the hill and not at the summit?

. . .

Every night a new realization, a new bruise
mottling the lack.

. . .

My sister says she would do what the man did. That's dumb,
says my brother. The baby had a life jacket on. In those temps
he could last a good thirty minutes.

. . .

Now the only one who knows how to navigate
is in the water without a vest, the muscles
necessary to keep his head above the waterline
quickly numbing.

. . .

In the newest rooms at the school for the deaf
the floors built to convey someone's entering.

. . .

What I would leap out of the boat for: the occlusion opening
straight to my heart.

. . .

I wrap what little I still have left
around the bar of my spine, imagine
feeling someone's footsteps
moving longingly toward me.

. . .

Did the man and his baby live?

. . .

What will the note say when at last
it is deciphered?

. . .

I am in a place in life
where I need to believe it is possible
to be rescued, to be pulled
toward a surface, toward light.

. . .

This is still a world in which five times out of ten
how could they not?

. . .

Finally you went to the fence and put your arm
through the links. You placed your thumb
on the skin in between my eyes—
an improvisation, the sudden unblocking of.

. . .

Each time it issued from the hole
in your face, my name like a piece of the godhead.

90° AND IT'S STILL ONLY SPRING

I paint my nails mint in an attempt to cool myself.
High winds and the Strawberry moon paddle is canceled.
At the all-day retreat at Deer Park, the lama tells us
we must wish that all sentient beings have the tools
to achieve happiness. Bub, look around, I silently think.
We are of a nature to burn. We have not gone beyond burning.
Behind me, the kid with the prayer wheel like a god with a world.

I AM PRO-LIVING BECAUSE

I believe in the heart. I believe we are all inter-connected. Webs within webs within webs. Each moment of intersection jeweled and shining, sacred. I believe in the oak, the wonder of its green canopy here on Earth. I believe in the body's intelligence. I believe I know what's best for me. I believe in community. I believe in strengthening the human family, which means caring for mothers and children, children whose birthright includes healthcare, daycare, food security, body dignity, clean air, pristine waters, education, adults who make a living wage. I believe in cultural vibrancy. I do not believe in darkness or in shame. I believe there is a difference between life and true embodied living. I have faith in individual agency as guided by our inner light and/or our god/s. I believe in empowering this light to shine even brighter. I believe the only absolute is love.

THE MAN ON THE TV IN THE BORDER TOWN SAYS HE FEELS NOTHING FOR THEM (PART 1)

It was just after lunch in the yellow room
when I wouldn't get out of the car
& how pleased my grandmother was made

by this news, wrapping her arms around me
as I sat there in the front
between her & Grandpa

as they did what they threatened they would do—
they took me home with them,
past the Point of Pines

where the planes come down over Boston Harbor.
Just the other night
I dreamed of the two of them

happy & shining as I threw
the blue blanket over their bed.
It was good to see them, to be reminded

of the afternoon when I was four
& I crawled in their car after lunch
& would not be moved

& so they took me home to Winthrop
just east of Boston where my grandmother
floated happily around the kitchen

as there was a child in the house again,
the feel of her hand on the back of my neck,
a presence I can feel even now when I am still.

But later after the sun went down,
a child of four, I missed my home,
my brothers, my sisters, my dog,

the lion quilt my mother hand-sewed for me
that I slept under each night,
& so my parents were summoned

to drive through the dark & come & get me,
& they did, they do, they will,
they are coming even now through this

terrible dark, child, they are coming
with all of their love & all of their hope,
with everything they are, they are coming,

please believe we are coming for you
even if the world would have you believe
we aren't.

REFUGE

Neither the estrangement
nor the homecoming,
nor the four dormant
orchids on the sill.
Not glitter or the dust,
exegesis or wonder,
the unfathomable love
stilled at land's end.
Not the resistance, the doubt,
the unchecked box, the rejection,
the heart's soft crown
left slightly puckered by the scar.
Not nights in the interminable dark
down on the knees.
Not the story or the afterimage,
light streaming around the body,
its grim pilgrimage.
Not what is. Not what isn't.
Neither air nor the void.
Neither the here nor the there.
Just this.

ROUGH AIR

Sometime around forty I said: soon
I'm going to give all this up—
the need to be elsewhere
as if *elsewhere* is better.
. . .

E.g. the night in Hoi An in the hotel's storage closet,
the raw-eyed rat Marguerite was savvy enough
to save until morning.
. . .

So many nights, so many rats, so many storage closets,
so many hours lazing around O'Hare, so many free socks and eye-
    shades,
so many movies on screens barely bigger
than a calculator, so many questions, so many in-flight regrets,
so many panic attacks at the idea I might have done it again,
left something on, a house burning down in the middle of the day,
so much wanting to be home already, wanting the journey to be over
but knowing that perfect story / perfect image
is out there, *elsewhere*, waiting
for me to stumble toward naming it.
. . .

E.g. the moon rising over the Indian Ocean
our first night on the catamaran,
the full moon hued like a fish egg
and calling for a sacrifice, demanding
you acknowledge her with whosever blood
you hold most dear.
. . .

As if a thing needs to be named in order to exist. I used to think this
until I saw a world without names, the emptiness of it,

the perfection. No, a thing only needs to be named
in order to be pulled out of what already is, wholeness,
and positioned in the story.

. . .

E.g. how I couldn't stop staring at the horns of light
protruding from Moses forehead, a mistranslation
resulting in the man being rendered a satyr, something cloven
and heavily furred, undying not because he chooses not to die
but because he can't.

. . .

Now they say don't use guidebooks, bring your own
fork and knife, stay longer in one place, hire local people,
eat what they eat, do what they do, blend in, roll
your clothes, pack out what you brought in,
don't go in the first place
though if you do, remember
why you're there, have a solid reason for being *elsewhere*
that'll stand up over time,
the magnificent sunsets like blood slowly leaking into a sealed space
not good enough.

. . .

Admittedly the outdated way of thinking (compulsion?)
leaked onward for a time
through many spaces.

. . .

E.g. the beautiful birthday cake they brought me,
the thing exquisitely frosted with my name
on it and a circle of candles,
yet when I cut into it, there was a strangely fibrous quality,
like a stack of fall leaves glued together,

the whole camp in hysterics, the thing
a cake-shaped mound
of dried elephant dung.

. . .

E.g. the waves twenty to thirty feet yet the race
wasn't canceled. The next day in the paper
stories of three separate incidents at various Sydney beaches
of swimmers with their necks broken,
the water lifting them in its indifferent jaws
and holding them aloft for what I imagine was one
shatteringly glorious moment.

. . .

Eg. for the cost of a local call, Alan picking up the payphone
in Esperanza, the Antarctic research station,
and ringing Buenos Aires.

. . .

Eg. the terrible capacity that revealed itself in me
along the beach road in G., the gun raised
above my head as if he would hit me with it
and I felt this thing come forward in me for the first time,
a knowledge that I have within me the power to die
and that one day I will use it.

. . .

Let's talk about how I came into being. Let's acknowledge
my status as the supplement, consequently the one
left exposed on the mountainside, the daughter
born in the Year of the Horse, the one who sets fires,
who needs to keep moving, an anticipater
who needs to remain in a state of anticipation.

. . .

Sound like anyone you know?

. . .

E.g. Because of my clothing nobody guessed I was one of them,
on Pham Ngu Lao the Southeast Asian sun defoliating the morning,
Pham Ngu Lao where I met the "sisters" who tried to scam me
not because I'm overly scammable but because in foreign spaces
I am someone who, should you wave me over, will walk into your home
and down a shot of whatever you hand me
and then walk back out into the Southeast Asian sun right as rain,
feeling good about being the kind of person
who will walk into a stranger's home and down a shot
of whatever is offered without question, the more unfamiliar the glass
the better, wine dark as soy, salty as blood
to the point where you wonder if maybe there was blood in it.

. . .

My favorite Camus (paraphrased): the only moral problem
is the problem of suicide, thus the meaning of life
is to live.

. . .

Bottoms up!

. . .

So many summers spent living like this, *elsewhere*
in the markets the animals stacked in cages,
everywhere cobras thick and blanched in the wine,
the snakes like bottled jewels, their eyes
left colorless which in my world means
they see all.

. . .

70

Camus again, this time in Oran, the pleasure he found
in the fights, in men struggling to be recognized
by their fists.

. . .

But on the other hand there's Gandhi
(always Gandhi!) with his second deadly sin: *pleasure
without conscience,* which describes so much
of the way this world wants me to live
and to which I gamely acquiesce.

. . .

A long time ago before I began to look *elsewhere*
I waded out with a paddle into waters
I'd come-of-age in, tried to heft a feathery body
up onto shore, but the thing was bloated
with negation—I could see the long
ragged gash where a boat had torn it open, set it
drifting. Thus I began to cry.

. . .

E.g. in Delphi, the solar god and his followers
are many because language itself
is multiplicitious.

. . .

I haven't stopped since.

. . .

Think of Apollo in all
his peregrinations—hunter, interloper,
warrior, exegete, the pythoness
stoned and riddling on the tripod,
the dactylic hexameter discursive

as possibility. *Today a great battle*
will be won. Cave of a hundred mouths.
Prince of Semiotics. The God of Truth
who deconstructs truth, the laurel
the symbol of his ambiguity, his failure
to heal even himself of love.

. . .

Admittedly in Delphi it was mostly about imagining
the hall of gifts, the fumes, the priestess
stoned time out of mind
as there wasn't much to see
at what was once the navel of the world.

. . .

What powered me over the continents?
Curiosity? Hubris? Thirst? Agency? What were the benefits
of staying in motion? How was travel a proxy
for seeking, as if to say,
"I'm not fond of this story, what else
you got?" the remote control forever gripped
like a sacred text?

. . .

What I believed: a true traveler can never be consumed, lose herself
to a god's mania
as you can never be caught
if you simply keep moving
like water flowing over the flanks of a shark, oxygenating it.

. . .

I didn't ever have to look within as I was preoccupied
with looking out.

. . .

I had thought this way of relating
meant no transcendence, none of that kind of happiness, the being strictly
without connection, and yes,
I was / am okay with that.
Truly.

. . .

Turbulence occurs due to wind, rising air, the jet stream, mountains,
another plane's wake. It's my favorite part
of flying, the feeling of the total loss of control.

. . .

The man who is tired of staying at home, often goes out abroad
from his great mansion, and suddenly returns again,
for indeed abroad he feels no better.

. . .

What I came away with when I finally stopped and looked:
the true power of the total abnegation
of hope.

. . .

—Lucretius, "On the Nature of Things"

. . .

E.g standing on a street corner in Dakar, smelling the same tear gas
I smelled in Madison, the Wisconsin air scorched unbreathable
in the name of property.

. . .

Perhaps there is still something to be said
for travel. If we only extended our meaning of the world *family*,
we would all be home by now.

BLACK PASTORAL

So why not live like that, what Michael
thought I meant when I said
the squirrel holds onto nothing

even as it buries its unburnished gold
in the dark? Why not be the soft paw
that turns the earth then yields, trusting

the thing will be there waiting, sustenance
for the winter road, or if not needed
will spark into this, these green capitals

under which we are hushed
and lifted up, called to testify
in these spaces that historically

have not made space for us?
Whose streets? Our streets.
Whose hills? Our hills.

Whose northern violets?
Whose red-tailed hawks?
Whose tall-grass prairie?

Our tall-grass prairie.
Our oak. Our spruce. Our ash.
Our broad-banded forest snails.

Our foxes red as rust.
Who keeps us safe?
We keep us safe.

Whose majesty and joy and struggle?
Whose voices rising in the growing light
on the mountain?

Who unlocks the gateless gate
and holds it open regardless?

IN THE SINE-SALOUM DELTA

Anytime one of the four of us—me, Masser,
the captain, his helper—leaned sideways,
you could feel it tip, your body
kiltering toward the place where on land
you would've fallen, the thing five meters long

and a little over a meter wide. I tried to imagine
fifty others crowded aboard, then fifty more
if the pirogue were slightly larger,
some with every important thing in a single bag,
others with just their souls clutched

to their chests, which is to say
their children. Masser says in the beginning
it was just boys, teenagers stealing a boat
at night and heading for the open sea,
Spain's Canary Islands a thousand miles away,

or maybe to Libya and then onto Italy.
And still they go, he says, though 4 out of 5 will die—
death by water, death by hunger, death
by lack of water, death by lack of a compass, death
by the hope of a hundred desperate people

and too little space. On the radio,
the most popular entertainer in Senegal
sings, "Last night in my dreams, all over the world:
food for all. Ça, c'est nécessaire," he concludes.
In the pirogue on the relatively glassy waters

of the Sine-Saloum delta, I lean east,
and the four of us lean east. Then someone leans west,
and whether we want to or not
we all lean west toward the setting sun.

"Apartment A, Unit 2" was written at the request of the Madison Museum of Contemporary Art in response to the work of artist Do Ho Suh.

If my memory of a dharma talk I heard once long ago is correct, then the Theravadan monk in the poem "By the Shore of Lake Monona, This is What I Heard" is Ajahn Amaro.

In the poem "In the Family" the young activist is the poet Danez Smith. I also quote the poem "Please Call Me by My True Names," which was written by the Vietnamese monk Thich Nhat Hanh, who passed in early 2022 and was often simply called Thay ("teacher").

The quote in "Foreward" is from Milton Mayer's book *They Thought They Were Free: The Germans, 1933–45*.

The idea for "Das und Das Pocket Field Guide to Occupied Lands" came from a visit to Vienna's Museum of Military History where I saw an exhibit of early twentieth-century pocket-sized field guides published for soldiers. These books were meant to give an invading army information about the people they would be encountering, but the texts were filled with misinformation and sensational propaganda meant to dehumanize the occupied populations.

The poem "Resurrection Theory" was published in the *Columbia Review* and was inspired by and borrows from the medievalist Lisa H. Cooper's 2004 talk "Craft for the Mastery: Divinity and Domestic Violence in *The Smyth and His Dame*." The italicized quote is from *A treatyse of the smyth which that forged him a new dame*, in *Altenglische Legenden mit Enleitung und Anmerkungen*, edited by Carl Horstmann. To read more about this work, please see Cooper's book *Artisans and Narrative Craft in Late Medieval England* (Cambridge: Cambridge University Press, 2011), 93–105.

The poet-priest quoted in "Unrequited Nocturne as Dream" is Spencer Reece from his book *The Road to Emmaus*.

Parts of the poem "Rough Air" have been published in slightly different forms in various journals.

"Black Pastoral" was commissioned by American Players Theater as part of their "If These Woods Could Speak" fall 2020 interactive event. In the penultimate stanza there's an allusion to "The Song of Amergin."

ACKNOWLEDGMENTS

A heartfelt thank you to the following institutions and residencies that helped support the writing of this work: Macdowell, Yaddo, the Bogliasco Foundation, the Rowland Writers Retreat, and the University of Wisconsin-Madison.